Night
Fishing

Story by Clare Scott

Illustrations by Liz Alger

D1377501

Rigby PM Plus Chapter Books
part of the Rigby PM Program
Sapphire Level

Harcourt Achieve Inc.
10801 N. MoPac Expressway
Building #3
Austin, TX 78759
www.harcourtachieve.com

10 9 8 7 6 5
09

Printed in China by 1010 Printing International Ltd.

Night Fishing
ISBN 0 75786 934 3

Contents

Chapter 1
The *Markita* Leaves the Harbor

"Is that everything, Nat?" Dad called as he stowed the fishing rods in the bow of their sturdy cabin boat, *Markita*. Nat and her father were preparing for a night's fishing.

"I think so," she answered. "Life jackets, spare clothes, towels, sleeping bags, bait, flashlight, and best of all, lots of food and drinks!"

Nat and her father often went out together on the boat — sometimes with friends, sometimes just the two of them — but they were always very careful.

"Always respect the sea," Dad would say. "It makes a great master but a terrible servant!" He would never go out without first checking the tides and weather forecast or testing the motor.

"Right! Flares, anchor, radio, full tank of gas, oars, charts, and bucket — all present and accounted for, Captain!" said Dad, pretending to salute. "I think that's it, then. We're off to feed the fishes!"

The sea was glassy calm as they eased the *Markita* away from the mooring. The sun was still burning hot, despite it being early evening. Sparkles danced on the rippling water, and the sky was a vivid blue with scatterings of fluffy clouds.

"Perfect!" said Dad with a satisfied grin. "This will be a great night. Look at that sea! Look at that sky!"

"Look at those boats!" said Nat, amazed. The ocean was alive with every variety of motor or sail boat, with large and small launches, and with yachts. They passed several kayaks and jet skis on their way out of the marina.

"Life jacket on?" asked Dad. "Ready for action?"

Nat smiled, gripping the seat tightly. "You know me, Dad. I'm always ready for action!"

Chapter 2
Dolphins on the Bow

Dad gradually increased the throttle, and the big outboard burst into life. The bow of the boat rose as it skipped over the waves, churning a frothy white trail.

"Yeehaa!" yelled Nat, grinning from ear-to-ear. She loved the feeling of the tugging sea-breeze and the salty spray on her face.

"We'll stay near Gull Rock tonight," Dad said.

Nat found it on the chart and shouted, "How long will it take us to get there? I'm hungry already!"

"About half an hour," answered Dad, "and you're always hungry!"

The *Markita* passed many boats, and the crews waved happily to each other.

"No traffic jams out here, Dad!"

"Yea, you're right! Wow, look at that!" Dad gazed admiringly as a huge, sleek yacht glided silently past. "Hey, Nat. Quickly!" Dad pointed as a variety of dark shapes appeared, flashing through the water beside them.

"Dolphins," yelled Nat. "Beautiful!"

9

The mammals kept pace with the boat, water droplets glistening on their arching backs. When Dad slowed, they slowed. When Dad sped up, they sped up. Most raced near the bow, but a mother and baby stayed alongside.

"Dad! She's smiling at me. Look!"

"She's showing off her beautiful baby to you, just like any proud mom."

Nat and Dad were fascinated by the dolphins' antics as they darted playfully through the water. Eventually the dolphins tired of playing and sped off, effortlessly bounding the waves.

"How cool!" yelled Nat, as the *Markita* picked up speed again.

Shortly, Dad pointed the boat toward a flock of diving birds.

"Gulls," he said. "You can tell by their V-shaped tails."

The sea was boiling with activity as fish frantically surged to the surface.

"The small fish are being chased by the big fish," explained Dad. "That's pretty exciting."

"Even more exciting if you're the one being chased. Quick, Dad, put out the lines!"

"Too late!" As Dad spoke, the activity ceased and the birds flew away, squawking angrily.

Dad increased speed again and the *Markita* surged ahead.

"Nearly there now," he shouted over the motor's noise. "Then we'll anchor and do some serious fishing."

"And eating!" added Nat.

Dad smiled as the *Markita* drove through the swell. "Sounds good to me!"

Chapter 3
Fishing at Sunset

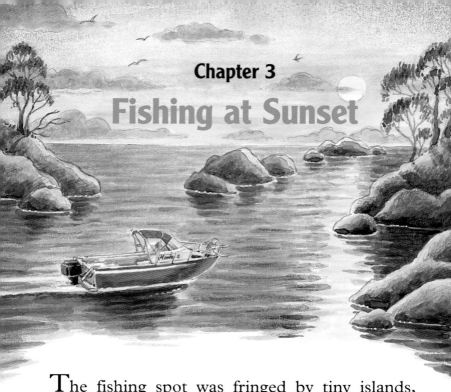

The fishing spot was fringed by tiny islands, some not more than rocky outcrops. As the *Markita* slowed and stopped, Nat eased down the anchor. As it settled firmly in the deep water, she gazed around. No other boats were visible, and the only other signs of life were distant sea birds.

The *Markita* swung around, facing into the breeze. Soon the only sounds were the water gently lapping on the hull and the occasional muted cracklings of the radio.

Dad sighed happily. "Listen!"

"Listen to what? I can't hear anything!"

"Exactly! Isn't it great?"

"Well, I guess it's better than squealing tires and sirens, anyway!"

Nat dragged out the picnic basket. "Now can we eat? Otherwise my stomach rumbling will spoil the quiet!"

Dad was already busy organizing the fishing gear. "As soon as we've got these lines out. I'll bait up while you throw some scraps for the fish. Then you can put out some food and drinks. That'll bring the fish. It never fails!"

Dad's prediction was correct. The urgent screaming of reels, and Nat's excited yells every time her rod jerked, frequently disrupted their meal. Several small fish were gently released.

"I hope you haven't forgotten our one rule of fishing," said Dad, trying to look stern, as Nat whooped with excitement at her latest catch.

They yelled in unison, laughing. "Whatever happens, never ever outfish the skipper!"

16

The golden sun sank lower into the sky, tucking itself behind a long cloud bank.

"Wow, what a sunset!" Nat briefly forgot the rods as she watched, transfixed. With night's onset and the turning of the tide, the fishing frenzy had eased. The sky rapidly darkened to an inky black, with millions of twinkling pinpoints. Occasional shimmers of sunlight reflections punctuated the water's surface. Nat strained her eyes, trying to make out shapes in the distance. But the night was so black and so still, it was hopeless.

"This is the best part. No lights, no noise — just us and the darkest dark!"

17

Dad fumbled inside the cabin with the flashlight, then switched on a small white light at the top of the boat.

"Oh, Dad!" Nat grumbled. "You ruined my night vision!"

"It's too dangerous not to have the riding light on, Nat. You know that. If another boat came along, it would never see us. Now, can you remember if the red light is on our port or starboard side?"

"Red is port, or left. Green is starboard, or right."

Dad pushed the switch for the other lights. "Very good. Now no one can miss us!"

"Well, I think it will be bedtime for us very soon." Dad yawned. "You must be tired. I know I am!"

"Can we just fish for a little bit longer? Please, Dad?"

"Well, okay, but not too long. I'll just clean up this cabin while you sort out those fish. Then we'll get some sleep so we can be ready for an early morning start."

Chapter 4

Mayday! Mayday!

Dad stowed the food and left the mobile phone handy. Unrolling the sleeping bags, he listened to the marine forecast again before turning down the radio and switching off the cabin light.

Suddenly Nat's rod began pulling frantically, the reel screaming. "Dad! It's huge! I can't hold it! Hurry! Dad ..."

Hearing Nat's urgent voice, Dad quickly stood up. In the darkness, he misjudged and hit his head violently on the cabin roof. With a soft moan, he collapsed in a heap.

"Dad!" Nat screamed, struggling to hold the rod. "Hurry up! What are you doing?"

Her grip slipped and she watched in dismay as her prized rod instantly disappeared into the blackness.

"Oh no! Now look what's happened! Dad! Dad?" Hearing no reply, Nat's voice changed from anger to fear. Looking toward the cabin, she could just make out a slumped form on the floor.

Nat rushed to her father and shook him frantically, but he didn't move. "This isn't funny, Dad. Stop joking!" she commanded.

But there was still no response.

Grabbing the flashlight, Nat was horrified to see blood coming down her father's ashen face.

Realizing what a frightening situation she was in, Nat began to tremble. She shouted for help, but her voice just echoed across the water. Nat had never been so alone and terrified in her entire life!

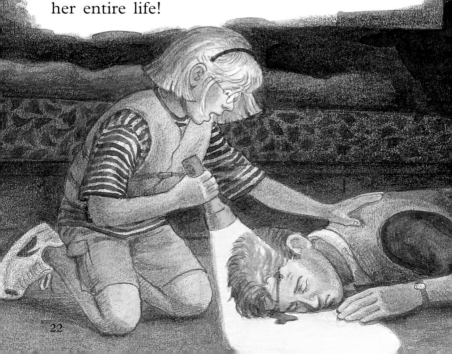

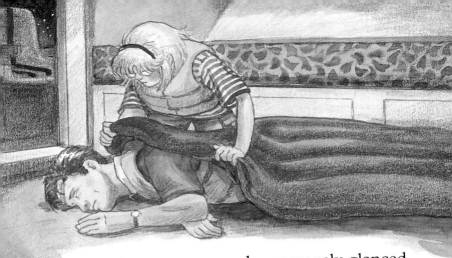

Brushing away tears, she nervously glanced at her father. He remained still and unresponsive.

"Think, Nat, think!" she ordered, taking several deep breaths. Turning on the cabin lights, she bent down to check him.

"A, B, C — Airway, Breathing, Circulation," she reminded herself, thankful of the first-aid course she'd recently completed at school. The only obvious injury was the head wound, but Dad was still unconscious.

His breathing was regular and he was lying on his side, so Nat covered him with a sleeping bag. Then she tucked a towel firmly around the cut.

"Must get help!" she muttered. Nat's hands were shaking as she picked up the mobile phone. Her emergency call wouldn't go through.

A crackle from the radio jolted her memory. "Of course! Channel 16 is the distress channel. I remember Dad showing me!"

Nat fumbled as she picked up the handset, desperately pushing in the button to transmit a message. "Mayday! Mayday! This is the *Markita*! Can anyone hear me? I need help urgently! Over."

Chapter 5

A Flare into the Sky

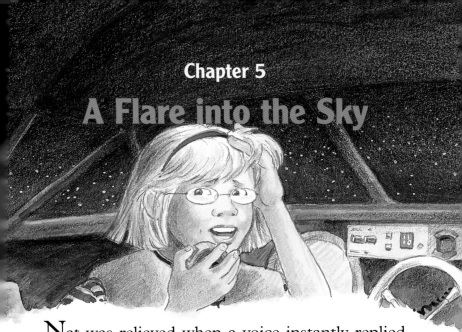

Nat was relieved when a voice instantly replied. "*Markita, Markita,* this is the coast guard. What is your problem and your position? Over."

Nat glanced fearfully at her father. "Coast guard, this is the *Markita.* We're anchored off Gull Rock and my dad's hurt himself. He's unconscious and I'm on my own. Please hurry! Over."

"*Markita, Markita,* this is the coast guard. We have dispatched the rescue helicopter. E.T.A. is 10 minutes. We have other boats in the vicinity en route. Do you have lights and flares? Over."

Nat reached into a cabin locker and pulled out a tin containing a variety of flares.

"Coast guard, this is the *Markita*. Cabin lights and riding lights are on. I've got a flashlight and flares. Over."

"*Markita, Markita,* this is the coast guard. Are you able to fire your flares? Over."

"Coast guard, this is the *Markita*. I think so. Over." This was one time Nat was extremely grateful for Dad's safety lessons.

"*Markita, Markita,* this is the coast guard. Fire your rocket flare now. Over."

Nat clambered out of the cabin to the middle of the deck. Gritting her teeth, she positioned the flare and pulled the pin. She felt a surge of relief as the flare forcefully shot high into the air, its bright orange glow lighting the inky sky.

"Coast guard, this is the *Markita*. I've done it. Now what? Over."

"*Markita, Markita,* this is the coast guard. You are doing a great job! Now, listen for other boats or the chopper. Be ready to signal them with a handflare or your flashlight. What's the condition of the patient? Over."

Nat quickly checked her father, willing him to respond. "Come on, Dad," she pleaded. "I need you. Wake up. Please wake up!"

But there was still no response.

Nat's voice trembled as she replied. "Coast guard, this is the *Markita.* There's no change. Over."

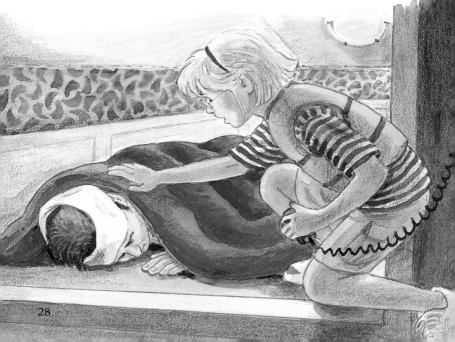

Chapter 6
Lifted to Safety

The coast guard officer continued to reassure Nat. Finally, after what seemed a lifetime, she heard the welcoming sound of the helicopter. Following instructions, Nat fired a handflare to identify the *Markita*, and soon her rescuers were directly overhead.

The forceful downdraft from the blades caused the *Markita* to bounce and fight the sudden uprising of waves, but a paramedic was safely lowered down to the deck.

Nat was so relieved to finally see help arrive that her knees gave way and she felt tears filling up in her eyes.

"Looks like you've got the situation all under control!" said the paramedic admiringly. "You've done everything right. Now you can rest and let me take over!"

As the paramedic treated her father, a coast guard boat arrived, and suddenly the sea was alive with concerned onlookers.

Nat watched anxiously as her dad was secured onto the stretcher, then raised up into the helicopter which was swinging high above the boat.

Suddenly she felt exhausted, as the events and emotions of the day finally caught up with her. The paramedic reassuringly patted Nat on her back.

"Your dad's going to be fine, Nat. It doesn't look serious, but we'll get him to the hospital for treatment. Do you want to come in the chopper with him or stay with the boat? The coast guard boat will tow it back to the marina."

"I'll stay with Dad, if that's okay," she said quietly, still worried about her father.

"No problem," he said. "We'll have you up with your dad in no time."

The paramedic fastened Nat securely into the safety harness. "You did a superb job. The least we can do is give you a chopper ride. Your dad will be very proud of you!"

He checked the last safety clip and gave the other paramedic the "thumbs-up" signal.

"Now, Nat, are you ready for action?"

As the harness tightened and Nat swung up off the *Markita*, she smiled nervously.

"I'm always ready for action!"